Roy Sheppard

Centre Publishing

First published 2002 by Centre Publishing, Somerset, England.
Re-printed 2003 and 2004

A catalogue record of this book is available from the British Library.

ISBN 1-901-53405-7
Book design and typesetting by Antony Parselle

Printed and bound in England by Biddles Ltd

Table of Contents

Introduction

Everyone involved in putting together business events puts massive time and effort into making it worth you being there. The most professional event organisers endeavour to leave nothing to chance.

And then you turn up! Ultimately, what you get out of an event is largely down to you. Your attitude and expectations can have a profound impact on the 'take home' value you receive.

Do you think ahead about what you want from it - or do you just show up - and 'see what happens'? A laid back approach certainly has its appeal but it won't necessarily help you - or those paying for your attendance. Events can be costly. The pressure is on to ensure they deliver tangible benefits to you and the organisers.

Can you afford to waste your precious time? Almost certainly not.

As someone who attends conferences professionally, I have met countless individuals who tell me that the key benefit of attending is the awesome networking opportunity. It's about the people they meet in the corridors, during lunch and dinner and in the bar at three in the morning.

However, so many of these intelligent, experienced and successful business people feel very uncomfortable walking into a room of strangers. They realise the need to do it, but quite a few feel gut-wrenchingly awkward about it. Initiating conversations frightens them. They don't know what to say. They worry about not remembering people's names. They know they need to circulate, but need some pointers on the art of conversation, and never feel good about extricating themselves when they have come to a natural end. What do you do? All of these 'afflictions' are more common than you would imagine. If you are a sufferer - trust me - you are in the majority. Therefore there is nothing wrong with you!

If you identify with any of the following comments, you will gain even more from what this book offers.

- *"I don't like the idea of 'schmoozing'at events."*
- *" feel a bit uncomfortable talking to strangers."*
- *"I just hate it when someone 'networks' me."*
- *"I only go to events when I absolutely have to. They tend to take up too much time - and I never get anything out of them any way."*
- *"I tried 'networking' last Wednesday - it doesn't work!"*
- *"Events are a great opportunity to meet up with old friends - I don't need to meet 'new'people."*

'Networking', 'schmoozing' and 'working a room' have become dirty words, conjuring up images of insincere, self-serving 'sharks' circling their prey. It's not nice when a stranger moves in on you and opens with, *"What would your wife live on if you died suddenly?"* These people are REALLY bad at networking. Inexperienced salesmen throughout the business world (not just insurance salespeople) fail to grasp the difference between crass selling and networking. It devalues them and fellow professionals within their industry, and influences the way their victims will feel about reaching out to meet new people in the future. Their approach is the equivalent of face-to-face junk mail. 99 out of 100 reject their offer. There is a better way.

This is why you will find hundreds of practical ideas in this handy pocket book, arranged in simple, easy and quick to read bullet points. Master these tips and you will improve your effectiveness at meeting new people at business and social events.

Perhaps you are a 'quiet' type. If so, you have even more potential to be good at this stuff. Whatever beliefs you have about networking will determine the decisions you take, the way you respond to networking opportunities and how you behave at networking events.

No matter how confident or proficient you may be at 'working a room', you will certainly gain from the insights within these pages.

Business 'leaders' realise something that 'followers' don't; 'know who' is more important than 'know how'. The most successful people are almost always the best connected. When you know the right people, you can always get the most up to date and relevant information. Followers mistakenly believe that the quality of their work is enough. It isn't. Mistakenly, too many bright people are convinced that their intelligence, education, skill, ambition and knowledge is all they need. What they fail to realise is that everyone else within their chosen profession is also bright, skilful and equally ambitious.

Another huge career mistake is to believe there

isn't enough time to build relationships with colleagues, customers and others in your industry. Find the time, get out more and apply this knowledge.

Your human capital (qualifications, experience and skill) is certainly important - but your social capital will open doors for you, quicker and more easily than through 'official' channels. It's all about who you know and who you can influence - your customers, clients, colleagues, competitors, suppliers, advisers and other contacts.

Although no pocket book of this size can include everything, this book has been designed to be read in less than one hour and will show you how to become someone who is better known, liked, trusted and valued. An excellent personal and professional reputation will precede you. You will be known as someone who respects others and will be perceived as a person who is worth knowing.

Roy Sheppard
Bath, Somerset, England November 2002

Benefits to You and Your Company

◗ Being proactive about building relationships is often perceived as a personal skill, but it's far more. It's an organisational competence. A large and diverse network of contacts will increase the sales of your company, whilst saving time and money. Just imagine the power if all your colleagues did the same.

◗ Poorly connected companies (internally and externally) are at a disadvantage, believing they are too busy. They lose out and are slower to respond to market needs.

◗ You don't get to the top, other people put you there. As your career develops, qualifications and intelligence aren't always enough to reach the top or achieve your career goals. Your ability to relate and connect with others is far more important.

◗ The good and the great become so because other people recognise their goodness and greatness. Talent doesn't set these individuals apart, it's the focus they have placed on developing a reputation with key influencers from the earliest stages of their career.

◗ Building a reputation indirectly through networking is an essential part of building your reputation directly in the field you work. Networking provides a profile and the resources for future use. Be a long-term thinker, not just a short-term doer.

◗ Want up-to-date information about a major competitor? When you are well-connected, you always know who to call.

- Every time you meet someone new, your access to potentially valuable new people is multiplied by the number of people they know.
- You can never know too many people - those you know today and meet tomorrow have the power to transform your personal and business life. And you can do the same for them.
- Your contacts can provide you with guidance, support, inspiration, financial help, as well as access to powerful and influential people. Tapping into the knowledge within your network will make your life easier and more fulfilling.
- Predicting many of the resources you will need in the future, and using a clearly articulated relationship strategy, can find key suppliers and other resources before you need them. Doing so will enable you to negotiate better terms.
- With excellent connections you will hear about employment opportunities first.
- Better contacts give you access to information, clients or jobs.
- A Dutch study showed that well-connected managers earned more, were promoted faster and at a younger age than individuals who were not so well connected. Such people build reliable networks before they actually need them, when they need advice they almost always get a quick answer. They effectively *"Dig their well before they're thirsty"*.
- Personal connections improve the chances of securing a more senior job.
- During an economic downturn or when companies

are downsizing, your contacts will be your lifeline to other opportunities.

▮ People with good networks can better handle a crisis. A well-maintained and diverse network provides not only basic support, but access to an extensive range of resources providing answers or responses quickly enough to avert full-scale disasters. Their networks help them adapt more smoothly to change, they are far less likely to have to struggle on their own, be ground down by the weight of responsibility, or stressed out about the consequences of their decisions.

▮ At a conference where my talk was aimed at facilitating better internal networking for a large global consultancy, the partners accepted how essential their business systems were to the success of the company. When asked *"How do you gain most of your clients?"* the answer was *""Through the people we build relationships with."* *"If that's the case, why is there no company system for this?"* I asked. Silence.

Companies that lack a systematic approach to relationship building are demoting it to the status of a random variable - a self-propelled force capable of producing positive and negative outcomes - not a good way to run a business.

The great paradox of networking is that, although it brings great benefits, you cannot go after these benefits directly. They come from investing in people and relationships. By contributing to others you will be helped in return, often far in excess of what you would expect or predict - but not necessarily from the same people.

If your overture towards people is simply to get business, you will close far more minds than you will ever close deals.

Pause for Thought

When you know exactly who you want to meet or the particular type of people or services you are looking for, you will be far more ready and likely to network productively, than if you wander aimlessly into a sea of people.

Before you attend your next event, ask yourself these simple questions:

- Why am I here? If it was forced on you - move to the next question!
- What would make it worth the investment of my precious time?
- What new information will be most useful to me?
- What questions do I want answered by the speakers?
- Who can I contact ahead of time to arrange a brief meeting?
- What do I need to know about the key people there?
- What information will my non-attending colleagues appreciate?

A Few Pointers Towards Success

- Decide to be more proactive about meeting new contacts.
- If necessary, get out more - invest the time to do it.

- Although some of these tips may be obvious, ask yourself *"What do I do with this knowledge at the moment?"*

- Set out to achieve a target to meet, say, three new people before leaving any event and increase this number as your confidence and/or expertise grows. Remember, meeting people is always about quality not quantity.

- Stop spending the majority of time at events with people you already know. Don't shun any of your colleagues and friends, but focus more of your energies on meeting new people.

- Sit next to people you don't know at conferences - especially at events organised by your company.

- Engage others in conversation.

- When meeting someone new, savvy people ask themselves *"How useful is this person to my entire network?"* A poor networker asks *"What can this person do for me?"* The interesting point is: good networkers not only build an admirable reputation, they benefit more than those who take a self-centred approach.

- Demonstrate that you are someone who is or could be worth knowing.

- What do you need to do to be someone who is thought of as a great person to have around? Is it you or your position in the company that gets the invitations?

- Who do you know? And who knows you?

- Realise that you can become really good at this quite quickly, using the tips and strategies in this book -

even if you have always thought of yourself as 'too shy'. The benefits will certainly outweigh any initial concerns you may have.

What to do Next

▶ At certain events, between 10-20% of delegates/ guests don't turn up. Event planners refer to them as 'No Shows'. Woody Allen said *"80% of success is simply showing up."* If you say you're going to be there - be there. Your reputation is important. Become known as someone who is reliable. If you really can't attend due to something unavoidable, telephone to tell your hosts.

▶ Once you have confirmed that you will be attending, contact the organisers for a list of attendees. Most organisers will oblige, especially if you have paid to attend. Don't do this under the misguided belief that it will help you decide if it's worth going - that's very rude.

▶ Scan the delegate list for those you know already.

▶ Identify individuals you don't know but would like to meet. Call or email the people you know to say that you're looking forward to meeting them at this event, and ask if they know the people you would like to meet. Be honest and upfront about it. Offer to do the same for them. Repeat this to a few of your contacts and you will almost certainly have introductions to a few of the individuals you have identified.

▶ Do some research about them - ask colleagues. Visit their company website. You will appear far better informed if you can weave some of this information into conversation, but don't use your new-found information to bombard them with facts about themselves - you could come across as a 'stalker'!

- Preparation will help ease any pre-event jitters you may have.
- Even if introductions are not promised, you have made a connection and offered help to someone who will appreciate your consideration and you will be more likely to look forward to the event.
- If it's a social gathering, ask the host/ess who will be there. Who do they recommend you meet? Why? Would the host be willing to make an introduction?
- If you are attending as a team member, prepare and share mini-biographies on your 'targets', check and agree the 3 messages you wish to convey about your firm and, if possible, what information you wish to gather.
- Determine to find out enough about those you meet to help them in some way. This does not mean selling them your products or services!
- Think through what you would like help with. What advice/information are you looking for? New suppliers?

What to Take With You

- Business cards - lots of them. Obvious, but so many people 'forget' to take them to networking events.
- A small note pad/self-adhesive notes and a pen.
- A delegate list if you have one.
- Breath fresheners and deodorant (!)

▯ DO NOT take brochures or flyers about your company, products or services.

When You Arrive

▯ Arrive early whenever possible and get involved. Offer to help the organisers - it will give you something to take your mind off any nervousness you might have.
▯ Being a greeter at the registration table will ensure you meet everyone. Later, you will be seen as a friendly face. More people will start to talk to you.
▯ Ask the organiser to suggest people you should meet and ask to be introduced.
▯ Being early will make it easier to start conversations, as few will have 'paired up' at that stage. It's also likely that you and your conversation partner will be joined by other early arrivals. By the time the event gets into full swing you will have already met a handful of people.

Name Badges

▯ If given a badge, wear it. If you have your own, wear that. (More and more people get their badges specially made to include their company name or a slogan designed to provoke a conversation - some work better than others!)
▯ Wear your badge on your right side so when you shake hands your badge is in their direct line of sight.

◗ Don't peer at the badges of others (even if it's because you forgot your glasses!) - it can look as if you are trying to see if the person is important enough to talk to.

Walk into a Room with Confidence

Walking into a room of people you don't know can be intimidating. Anyone who feels particularly uncomfortable about it is less likely to go out of their way to get into such a position. This may protect you from feeling uncomfortable, but it won't help you meet new people. When you DO put yourself through such potential torture - it's so easy to give the situation far more attention and importance than it deserves. Guess what - a HUGE proportion of people feel uncomfortable about it. Odds are 5 out of every 6 people you are looking at feel uncomfortable at the prospect.

◗ Focus on putting other people at their ease. By choosing to act as a 'host', regardless of whether it's your event or not, you are actively concerned, not with your own discomfort, but with ensuring the comfort of others. You will forget about your own feelings.
◗ Look for people standing on their own and set yourself the task of helping them to feel better about being there.
◗ Word of warning. Sometimes you'll discover why they were on their own! If they turn out to be obnoxious, ignorant, arrogant or smelly - introduce them to someone else who you also know

to be similarly obnoxious! You will be doing everyone else a favour.

- Promise yourself that you won't think others don't want to talk to you just because they 'look' arrogant or aloof. Most of the time these people send out such vibes because they are feeling so shy and uncomfortable. Do you do that yourself?

- Similarly, just because someone doesn't look at you when you are in conversation, doesn't necessarily mean they are distrustful. Again it could be shyness.

- Here's a tip I learned from Anneka Rice, a UK TV personality with a reputation for being particularly gregarious. To overcome her extreme shyness early in her career she learned to take on the qualities of the people she admired for their confidence and charisma. By 'acting' like them she soon acquired those positive traits for herself. It works, give it a try. No-one need know that it's an act. Although a John Wayne walk could give it away!

- How confident you feel and how confident you look are not the same. If you don't feel particularly confident, learn to stand upright with your feet slightly apart, don't fold your arms, or cover your mouth with your hand, make eye contact with those around you and have a smile on your face - this doesn't mean you should grin like a Cheshire cat. Be welcoming not intimidating. Send out signals that you would welcome a conversation with others. This will increase the likelihood it will happen.

- Stand up. Sitting down at a networking event doesn't work.

First Introductions

▮ Whenever possible, identify people you want to meet before you arrive at the event.

▮ Once you have a list, identify people who know you and ask if they would be prepared to introduce you to anyone on your list. It's great if they know the person, but it isn't essential. Offer to do the same for them.

▮ Your introducer should state your full name - and your title - or a brief description of your job responsibility. Perhaps they could also add a comment about why you are so valued within your company, your specific knowledge/expertise or a recent success in which you have been instrumental.

▮ Explain that this will help establish your credibility more quickly with the person. Insist they do NOT say that you asked them to say this - even if they think it would be funny. This would effectively push you into a deep hole - the first few seconds of your meeting would then mean climbing unceremoniously out of it.

▮ Generally speaking you would introduce a junior TO a senior, a manager TO a director, a colleague TO a customer, client or guest.

Introducing Others

▮ Be proactive. Offer to introduce people. Your contacts will appreciate your consideration. All you have to do then is get it right.

- Ensure your introduction of colleagues highlights their talents and the importance of their contribution to your firm. In private, ask how they would like to be introduced. This improves the likelihood that you won't mis-introduce them.

- Decide who is being introduced to whom. Look at the person being introduced TO and say *"John, I'd like to introduce you to Jessica Russell. Jessica is regional sales manager with xyz company. Since she joined two years ago, Jessica has been responsible for a sales increase of x%. She's doing a great job and has become a real asset to the company. Before she joined us, she worked for 5 years with your friend Peter Wynn Davies and his team."*

- Then add *"Jessica, this is John Gommes, the new CEO at abc company. He was appointed because of his specific expertise within the x industry. I've known John for ten years - he's brilliant at spotting opportunities to apply technology."*

  Note how many times you have deliberately repeated each person's name within the introductions, to help both lodge the name in their memory banks. By saying something positive about them and their accomplishments you establish mutual credibility. You've set them up for a meaningful conversation.

- Sadly, the world of business is still populated by Neanderthal men who haven't quite grasped the fact that there are a growing number of highly competent women in the workplace. Too often men are introduced with their full name, job title and successes - while women colleagues get *"And this is*

Pam from our marketing department." 1) Pamela hates being called 'Pam' and 2) She's the senior marketing manager for the most profitable division of the company. Introduce everyone equally.

▮ If you are poorly introduced in this way, respond by saying *"Hello, yes, I'm Pamela* (with a slight stress on the full name) *Johnston, senior marketing manager in the xyz division."* Alternatively, early within the ensuing conversation you could say *"What I have found in my capacity as senior marketing manager for xyz division is...."*

▮ For a man, don't introduce female colleagues by referring to the way they look or what they wear. Leave that up to the person they have been introduced to.

Introducing Yourself

▮ Offer a warm smile. Extend your right hand in a warm yet quietly confident manner.

▮ Always offer your name first when starting a conversation. It's more likely to put people at ease when they know who they are speaking to.

▮ Offering your name first will often (but not always) trigger the other person to offer their name.

▮ When you meet someone you think you may have met before, state your name first - help them out. Assume they do not know or remember yours - it puts the other person at ease.

▮ If they don't offer their name and you can't remember it - be honest and say *"Didn't we meet at such and such place? I'm desperately trying to remember your name - please help me out."*

◗ Include in your self-introduction some 'conversational bait'. A brief comment about yourself, the situation or circumstances of your meeting that will help the other person begin a conversation.

Remembering People's Names

This is a major problem for a lot of people. The truth is - most of us don't pay enough attention when we are told someone's name. Too many things are buzzing through our minds such as *"what do I think of this person?"*, *"How are they dressed?"*, *"Why are they here?"*, *"How much am I attracted to them?"* (Our primitive brains sometimes have difficulty being politically correct!) Small wonder we don't always hear names when they are given.

◗ Develop the habit of really listening when people give you their name. Silence that inner voice.
◗ Whenever someone gives their name imagine that you will be called upon to introduce this person within the next 10 minutes. This often happens anyway! By taking this approach you will be far more likely to put the necessary effort into remembering their name. Focus initially on memorising a first name if it helps.
◗ If you didn't catch the name the first time - ask for it to be repeated. It tells them that getting their name right is important to you.
◗ If the name is hard to understand because the person is from a different culture, ask them to spell it - or ask for their business card to see it written down.
◗ The best strategy for remembering names varies slight-

ly from person to person. We all have a preferred learning style and process information differently. Regardless of these apparent differences, psychologists agree that the more sensory channels we employ and the deeper the sensory imprint we form around a person's name, the greater our power of memory.

◗ Here are three memory strategies for remembering names. 1) Silently repeat their name and focus on the sounds of words. If it helps, explore the rhythms of the words and language. 2) Form visual associations to the names, observe any characteristics and create any symbols or images that will help you picture them and see their name in your mind. For example - Liam Fox could produce an image of a lamb chasing a fox. Is there something unique about the way they look to use as a memory hook to link to their name? 3) In addition to any silent repetition or pictures, think of a gesture or imagine a feeling or sensation that in some way symbolises the name or picture for you.

◗ Perhaps you are great at remembering names but fail to remember their face? Are you really looking at people in the first place? Where is your attention truly focused when you first meet people? Do you make eye contact long enough for you to register their face? Or perhaps you concentrate too much on their eyes at the expense of getting a wider picture of them as a person?

◗ People appreciate it when you remember them but readily accept it when you admit you haven't.

Helping Others to Remember You

▶ On stage as a speaker I wear a unique suit. The jacket is a 'frock coat' that reaches my knees. Some people dislike it. That's OK because it serves two important purposes - it gives me an opportunity to poke fun at myself (audiences always like to see someone who doesn't take themselves too seriously) and if someone can't remember my name, I get jobs from agents who have had a request for *"The guy who wears the funny coat."* Agents know who they are talking about.

▶ How do people remember YOU? It's important. You don't have to do anything outrageous.

▶ How you say your name can have a profound impact on how memorable you are. All too often, we don't exercise enough care when we say our own names. Don't mumble it. Slow down and speak clearly.

▶ Try this technique used by the actor John Wayne in his movies. When he delivered a line he would pause halfway through it. This has the effect of drawing the listener closer towards you, as you eagerly await the rest of the line. By using this technique - say *"Hello, my name is ... Roy Sheppard."* But please substitute your own name - don't use mine! It gives the listener time to concentrate on your name and it increases the likelihood they will remember it - your ultimate aim.

Confident Conversation

Conversation is a dance. You don't have to do all the steps. Imagine how stupid it would look if you tried. In a good conversation there is always enough space for each participant to have their say. A good conversationalist encourages others to speak and listens attentively to what is said, while poor conversationalists hog the spotlight. It's a cliché but we have two ears and one mouth - use them in that proportion.

- Not knowing what to say in a conversation is a common fear. Learning to be a better listener will help.
- Eager to present ourselves well, we often fall into the trap of trying to fill in the silences by talking about something we sound very knowledgeable about - namely ourselves or our business. Be more 'interested' rather than trying so hard to be 'interesting'. How much time do you spend thinking about what to say next - rather than really listening? By learning to ask intelligent, sensitive and sensible questions, rather than trying to impress them, you will impress them more. Actively encourage others to talk. You will be amazed at how interesting they will think you are.
- When starting or initiating a conversation with someone you don't yet know, focus on the potential benefits of talking to someone new, rather than how you could feel if they don't want to talk to you. Tell yourself before you start any new conversation *"This conversation has the power to lead to a lifetime friendship for me or some of the other people I know."*

- Consider any common ground people are likely to share, e.g. interests, their relationship to the host, reaction to professional, industry, national or international headlines, their journey to the event.
- Start with getting others to talk about themselves. What are they most enthusiastic about? What are their favourite things? What do they like to do when they are not working?
- Make a genuine and complimentary comment about those you meet.

Feel, Felt, Found is a useful conversational technique.

- FEEL: When your conversational partner has made a statement, if it's true - you might like to add *"I fully understand how you feel."*
- FELT: Share with the person how you felt the same way yourself.
- FOUND: Then share with them what you found that helped you move on, or deal with the situation.

Example: *"i know how you feel. It's a frustrating and an anxious time for you, wondering where you will be, post-merger. I remember three years ago, when our company downsized, I felt apprehensive every morning for five maybe six months in the lead up to the company announcement. Then I found that I got to the point where I said to myself that I wouldn't let the situation defeat my enthusiasm for the industry, and would ensure that I stayed ahead of trends and took far more interest in the health of the company, so such a blow wouldn't come as a shock again..."*

Feel, Felt, Found works best when it conveys expressions of genuine empathy rather than sympathy - if you cannot associate with how they feel, don't fake it.

Author Susan RoAne suggests adopting the OARs approach;

- O   Offer an observation
- A   Ask a question
- R   Reveal your thoughts, experiences, ideas, or opinions.

Revealing Ourselves

To be a HIT with those you meet, you need to demonstrate H - Honesty, I - Integrity and T - Trust. One way to achieve this is by revealing something about ourselves or even sharing our self-doubts or vulnerabilities. This does not mean turning your conversations into confessionals or counselling sessions.

- Someone asks you the common question *"How's business?"* It hasn't been good - or it's been terrible. What do you say? Honesty is often the better option. A friend of mine who runs a local hotel met with a competitor. She asked *"How's business?"* *"Oh great - really busy."* came the reply. The same question came back but rather than echo what had been said my friend said *"I'm delighted for you that business is so good - we've found it very quiet. Bookings are way down on last year."* The conversation was transformed. The competitor came clean and said her business was also suffering, although things had started to improve. Without the honesty, the conversation would have stayed on the polite but meaningless level. Obviously this doesn't always happen. But most people appreciate it when you cut the BS! It provides a solid base for a future relationship. Both hoteliers have become friends even though they are still competitors. They even feed business to each other when they are full.

📶 People may value you for what you know, but they will like and trust you for who you are.

The Power of Questions

📶 Ask lots of questions of the people you meet. You'll learn something.

📶 Ask open ended questions - those which include 'Who, what, where, when, why and how'. It's difficult to answer these with a simple 'yes' or 'no' - words which shut conversations down.

📶 Don't do this in such a way that they feel interrogated by you - just be interested.

📶 PLEASE NOTE. Asking personal questions is a sensitive issue. It is not always appropriate. Anyone who perceives you as someone who is 'pumping them for information' will distrust you. Building trust, rapport should be the aim at all times.

📶 By devoting even part of your time enquiring about others you begin to be seen as someone who has a genuine interest in them as a person, rather than just what they can do for you.

What do you ask? Bob Burg, in his book *Endless Referrals* suggests memorising these 10 questions:

1. How did you get started in your business?
2. What do you enjoy most about your profession?
3. What separates you and your company from your competition?
4. What advice would you give someone just starting in your line of business?
5. What one thing would you do with your business if you knew it could not fail?
6. What significant changes have you seen take place in your profession or business through the years?
7. What do you see as the coming trends in your business?
8. How would you describe the strangest or funniest incident you've experienced in your business?
9. What ways have you found to be the most effective for promoting your business?
10. What one sentence would you like others to use in describing your business?

These questions are practically guaranteed to get a conversation going with anyone who's in business. But what if you don't want to know anything about their business life - here are some more personal questions few should find too invasive:

1. Could you help me, when you go out to eat, where are your favourite restaurants for lunch or dinner around here? Asking for help is always a good opener. Asking for advice or easy to share information is also very effective.
2. What's the best thing about living around here?
3. Where were you born/brought up?
4. What would you like to be doing in five years, that you're not doing today?
5. If you could improve one area of your life - what would it be?
6. What's the best thing about your work?
7. What do you tend to do outside business?
8. What's your partner's name?
9. Do you have a family?
10. How old are they?
11. Who do you most admire? Why?
12. What do you most want out of life?
13. What has been your proudest moment so far in your life?
14. Is there anyone here you would like to meet?

You can probably think of many more questions that will help others talk enthusiastically about themselves and their businesses. This will provide you with a deep insight into what makes them tick - and unearth all sorts of ways you, or one of your contacts could help them. In a later section we will cover how you can follow up on what you have learned.

"And What Do You Do?"

Eventually, one question you will probably ask or be asked is *"And what do you do?"* There are two parts to this; asking and answering.

Personally, I try not to ask this question because it is potentially dangerous. Suppose the person says (this actually happened to me) *"I was made redundant four months ago. I can't find another job - and on top of all that my wife has left me and taken the children."* What would you do in such a situation? Offer a drink and walk away perhaps. Hardly. But neither is it your responsibility to be an unpaid therapist.

Some people also resent being asked what they do because it can sound as though they are being evaluated for their potential usefulness. Many think (rightly or wrongly) that those who initiate conversations have a hidden agenda - and they will be discarded if not 'important enough'. Talk to people as people NOT potential clients. It isn't about them anyway - but who they know - and what they may say about you to other influential people 'behind your back'. Find ways to be of value to everyone you meet regardless of their position in life. You can always find out what someone does later, after they have given you their business card.

Instead of asking what people do, wait until you receive their business card. Then it's perfectly acceptable to make a comment or ask questions about their responsibilities etc.

What if you are told *"Oh, I'm just a secretary."* Or *"I'm just a guest/housewife."* Too often support staff and partners or spouses feel out of place and uncomfortable at some corporate or business events - a golden opportunity to help them feel welcome. Look after them. Engage them in conversation. Treat them better than anyone else you ever meet. They are 'gatekeepers' and can wield enormous influence with key decision makers - treat them badly and they can and will refuse access. Stand out as someone who treats them well and your personal and professional reputation can be enhanced hugely. What are their interests? Their opinions? As ever, share your thoughts too - to ensure they don't suspect you are 'pumping them for information'.

I once asked a member of the audience what he did. He said *"I'm a venture capitalist."* I asked *"How do people generally respond to that?"* *"Come to think of it - they normally make for the bathroom or go to get a drink!"* came his reply. Howls of laughter from the rest of the group - all VCs working for the same firm. In some circumstances meeting a VC would be of enormous interest - but it's a specialist area that wouldn't always evoke enthusiasm. I suggested the following response: *"I help create millionaires."* Someone else said *"That won't work - it sounds like you work for the Lottery!"* I then explained how important it is to offer an answer that indicated a result you help to create, rather than simply name, rank and serial number information that won't interest the majority of the people you meet.

In an exercise to explore what they could say to the question, they came up with quite a selection. The most memorable were *"We help greedy bastards"* and *"We help middle aged men become more appealing to younger women."* Wouldn't that look so cool on the back of a corporate business card? For some reason they weren't convinced! But it certainly opened their minds to options and choices they have to engage people in conversation. More than one of those people have since told me that they now say those things in conversation at functions and parties - with huge success. They learned that my initial idea would have wide possibilities because it meant they could go on to explain that they identify businesses with high growth potential. They invest money in them, then in 3-5 years most do incredibly well - and turn the owners into millionaires! Their answer provides 'legs' for the ensuing conversation.

A tax accountant intrigues people with *"I collect brown envelopes."* And goes on to explain *"When the tax man sends my clients a brown envelope - I take it off their hands and sort it all out for them."* How would you respond if someone said *"I help people to pick their nose."* He quickly adds - *"I'm a plastic surgeon!"*

So, what result do you create? How can you succinctly encapsulate it in a way that a lay person will understand and be sufficiently interested to know a bit more? Sometimes known as an 'elevator speech' (how would you 'sell' the value of your company to a stranger if you only had the duration of a short elevator ride), it deserves careful thought. Perhaps you need a few alternatives for different groups. As an international conference moderator I say *"I'm a business Oprah Winfrey"* My consultancy is *"To our clients we are their business development department."*

- Don't use jargon. Brainstorm ideas with colleagues to intrigue or amuse.
- When your own introduction is well rehearsed (but not TOO well rehearsed), concise and geared towards showing people what results you provide your customers, you will come across as someone who knows what you are about and will project an air of self-confidence and enthusiasm.
- Try out different approaches with friends and colleagues to find out what works.
- The secret is saying something so that others want to know more about you.
- Being asked what you do should not be taken as permission to devote the rest of the conversation to your favourite subject!

Managing the Conversation Flow

- Do not use the opportunity to impress everyone with your superior knowledge by turning your comments into a mini presentation in its own right.
- Don't interrupt.
- Some people find it difficult to put across their ideas clearly - don't dismiss them just because they can't do it. Encourage them, but don't finish off people's sentences, especially if they have a speech impediment.
- Others don't want a conversation - just an audience. Bette Midler's character in the movie *Beaches* sums them up when she said *"Oh, enough about me. What do YOU think of me?"* When a grand-

stander pauses to take a breath, jump in to ask someone within the group for their thoughts on the topic. Facilitate a discussion by encouraging others to contribute. When the grandstander tries to regain 'centre stage' by interrupting, gently say to the person who was interrupted *"Please finish what you were saying."*

💠 Hold back on giving well-meaning advice during conversations, unless you are specifically asked for it. Especially avoid using the words 'you should'!

💠 If anyone gives you a compliment - quietly thank them. Do not brush their remark aside with a self-deprecating comment under the mistaken belief that you are demonstrating humility. It robs the other person of the satisfaction they get from giving the compliment. However, if you are mistakenly applauded for something achieved by someone else - give credit where it's due.

Breaking into a Group

Breaking into a group can be a daunting prospect especially if the conversation appears to be in full flow. Here are a few ideas to consider:

💠 Arrive early - a group is more likely to form around you.

💠 Find someone such as the organiser, a friend or a colleague to introduce you to the group.

💠 As long as you don't look like a waiter or waitress (dressed in black and white), offer a plate of food or drinks to the group you wish to become a part of. Then stay.

◗ If you are involved in a conversation with a small group of people and you see someone hovering on the out-skirts of the group, if you're not discussing something private or confidential, take the initiative to bring them into the discussion. Offer your name first and then ask theirs. Briefly summarise the conversation and intro-duce those who are present. If you do not know all of their names, don't be embarrassed - simply say that you don't know and allow them to introduce themselves - the chances are you will also be helping others in that circle who may be thinking - *"Thank goodness you've done that - I didn't have a clue who I've been talking to for the last 10 minutes - it would be too rude to ask now!"*

How and When to Offer Your Business Card

◗ If you don't already, start to carry your business cards with you everywhere you go. I distinctly remember speaking at a conference for eight hundred newly appointed senior managers of an international firm based in the US. I asked *"Who is carrying their busi-ness cards right now?"* 90% weren't. Why weren't they? They didn't think they needed to because it was 'just' an internal meeting.

◗ Your card is your ambassador, a cheap and nasty one says the same about you. A poorly designed and badly printed card will help to make you appear cheap and nasty too. If that's your style - fine - if it isn't - invest in decent cards.

- Carry spare business cards in your bag, briefcase, and in the glove compartment of your car.
- Discard any out-of-date business cards and have new ones designed and printed.
- Keep your cards in a particular pocket or the same place in your bag, so that you can retrieve one without having to make a big deal of it. Put all 'incoming cards' into a different pocket or a different place in your bag.
- Spraying your cards around like a tom cat is not regarded as professional behaviour.
- Don't be someone who passes out business cards to everyone, but doesn't know anybody.
- If you perform a number of different job functions - have different cards. If you are self-employed, rather than including what you do - just use your name. Your card will have wider usage.
- If you work for a large organisation, perhaps you could have different cards for internal and external use.
- Rather than offer your card when you first meet people, wait to be asked for it. When people ask you for your card, take it as a sign that they have seen that you could be potentially valuable to them. Until they ask - you have more work to do.
- If you have a unique or difficult name to pronounce or remember, offer your name slowly and clearly and then hand them your business card and say - *"I've found that most individuals have a problem with my name - so here's my card so you can see how it's spelled."* This way you are seen to be helping those you meet, rather than pushing your card on to them.

- Ask for cards near the end of a conversation and use your request as part of the process of bringing a conversation to a close. If you collect someone else's card and they don't ask for yours, they could be someone who doesn't see the value of building relationships or they are simply rude.

- Consider putting your photo on your card - it helps people remember you when they flick through their card collection. Rather than a boring head and shoulders shot, use something that shows you being active or doing your job.

- How about including on the back of your card, a brief summary of what results you or your company provides its customers?

- Add *"We met at...."* This allows you or the recipient of the card to add details of your meeting. This can help your contacts remember you more clearly.

- Even include on the back *"Please keep this card for reference or pass on to a colleague"*.

- One situation when it is good to offer your card before you are asked for yours - is when you offer tangible help that they would benefit from and appreciate - with NO personal benefit to you. Encourage the person to take you up on your offer by giving your card and insist they contact you for the help.

- Don't say goodbye to an interesting person unless you have their details. They can be written on the back of one of your cards (cross out the front to make sure you don't give it away to someone else).

- If someone is particularly interesting when you meet them ask for two cards.

When meeting people from Asia the following comments about exchanging business cards are worth noting: In Asia, offering and receiving cards is a formal ceremony.

◗ Don't casually offer your card with just one hand. Hold your card with both hands when you give it. Pass it the right way up so the other person can read it immediately.
◗ Don't write on business cards.
◗ Show respect when you receive a card by using both hands. Look at it, study it, then put it away carefully. Do not put it into your back pocket.
◗ More western companies are dispensing with job titles. Titles are important in Asia.

Body Language

◗ Don't invade the personal space of others. Unless forced to do so through a lack of space, stand no closer than 3 feet (1 metre) away from someone you don't know well.
◗ Become attuned to the body language and interest level of those around you - are they looking around, looking down, looking into their empty glass or giving you other non-verbal signals?
◗ Since you will be shaking hands with your right hand, you don't want it to be cold and wet. People form an impression of you within seconds, and a freezing cold handshake can create a negative impression. Hold cold drinks with your left hand, if you can.

The Different Conversation Styles of Men and Women

▶ After detailed research, Deborah Tannen, author of the book *You Just Don't Understand* found that men tend to 'report talk' while women 'rapport talk'. This means that men often give the outcome of a story first and then fill in the details. A significant proportion of women provide all the incidental details about who said what to whom and why, including lots of interesting observations along the way, eventually reaching the point of the story. Neither is right or wrong - they are just different approaches.

▶ For a man to build better rapport with women, adjust your language to include more rapport talk. While a woman who needs to build rapport with men, might be better off adopting a more report talk style.

▶ Too many men hog too many conversations. Men talking to men have learned how to handle this - they just butt in to make themselves heard. But for women, especially in a business context, to assert themselves whilst ensuring that they are not seen as being too pushy is a constant balancing act. Rightly or wrongly men like to talk about themselves - but many men perceive others who don't say much as not having anything worthwhile to contribute.

▶ What can a woman do to contribute to a conversation without being seen to hog the spotlight? It's all about questions again. Carefully phrased questions can easily be made to demonstrate your depth of knowledge, insight and dispel any suspicions that you don't know much.

When West Meets East

Cultural differences especially between the West and Asia, are worth mentioning. It's easy to offend without meaning to. Many Asians may be eager to adopt Western lifestyles, but being seen to respect such differences will be appreciated. This is a **MASSIVE** subject - the following information is included to help you be aware of just some of the many cultural differences.

- A handshake can last up to 10 - 15 seconds.
- The habit of touching or holding someone's arm when you speak is not regarded as friendly.
- For Muslims there is no physical contact between men and women.
- If you are a woman, it is not recommended to offer your hand to a Muslim man.
- Some men don't offer to shake the hands of women. If you are a woman, let them offer their hand to you.
- Kissing - even a peck on the cheek - is NOT polite or acceptable.
- The left hand is thought of as unclean, so don't pass things with the left.
- Pointing with your index finger is regarded as rude. With a left hand it's worse! This was pointed out (no pun intended) to me after the publication of my

book *Rapid Result Referrals*, featuring an extremely rude photo of me on the back cover! In Asia, you only point at animals.

- Nor should you ever beckon with a wagging finger.
- Moving your head side-to-side means agreement - for westerners it's disagreement!
- Standing with your hands on your hips is interpreted as anger and aggression.
- The head is sacred. It is where the soul is located so never touch anyone's head or pat the hair of a child.
- It is obscene to punch your fist into your own hand.
- Everyone knows that saving face is crucial in Asian culture. Giving face is important too. You will achieve much more by giving more credit than is perhaps deserved.
- Confrontation is to be avoided at all times.
- Ask how the person would like to be addressed.
- Leave time for people to respond to you. Silence is acceptable in many Asian cultures and is a sign of politeness.
- If you are ever given a gift, don't unwrap it in front of the person - it's rude. If the gift is inappropriate they will lose face.
- Be seen as someone who is open to learn.
- NEVER criticise the country, politics, government bureaucracy, religions or talk about sex.
- Don't talk about your own personal successes. This is rude and boastful.
- In Asian culture you will rarely hear anyone use a categorical *"No"*. *Yes,* does not automatically mean *Yes*, it could mean, *I agree, I hear what you say* or a *maybe*.

▶ A pause is sometimes a sign for 'No'. The person could be trying to think of a way of breaking 'No' to you gently!

▶ People who speak English as a second language have the luxury of choosing the words they use. When they listen, they don't choose the words. Therefore, they may sound more fluent than they are. Speak English slightly more slowly to non-native English speakers. Saying the same thing in different ways can also help.

We in the West could learn SO much from how important respect, harmony and relationships are in Asian culture. For more information on cultural differences, read *Communicating Across Cultures* by Phillip Khan-Panni & Deborah Swallow.

Exits from a Conversation with Style

All conversations come to a natural end - some sooner than others. Sadly, too many people wait and wait for others to do it for them! They're often afraid it will appear rude. It's not, when you do it respectfully. Many would rather stand around with nothing to say until somebody else decides to do the decent thing and put everyone out of their misery! So be brave - take the initiative. People will appreciate it.

▶ Act confidently - even if you don't feel that confident about taking the initiative to end a conversation.

- You don't have to resort to feeble excuses such as: *"Excuse me I need to visit the bathroom"*, *"I need to find my colleague"* , *"I need a drink/food."*
- Nor should you try spinning a line about needing to leave the event and then staying. They will almost certainly see you later happily chatting to someone else. What will that say to them about your integrity and honesty?
- After a while you may want to move on. Say that you don't want to impose too much on their time and ask which other people they think you should meet? Would they be prepared to introduce you?
- Alternatively you could offer to make an introduction to anyone they would like to meet. You don't actually have to know the person in question to do this.
- Honesty is by far the most effective (and least used) tactic. Say *"It's been a pleasure meeting you* (assuming it has); *I'd like to meet some more people, perhaps we can meet again"*. If you got on particularly well, it may be appropriate to get out your diaries and fix something up there and then.
- Make sure you have the other person's business card. If they don't have one, write the person's details on the back of your card or on a scrap of paper - making sure you spell the person's name correctly - better still ask them to write it all down for you - legibly.
- Invest in a small notebook for these situations and carry it with you everywhere. You can then add any relevant note about that person, or the gist of your conversation.
- Emergency exits. When attending with a spouse or colleague, try organising a secret code to alert each

other to unwanted attention. When they approach (or get called over) reaching out to gently squeeze their elbow in a particular way could be their cue to 'get me away from this person'.

▶ At the end of every conversation, do a brief mental audit - ask yourself who knows more about each other? Do you know more about them, or do they know more about you? If it's the latter all the time, perhaps you need to change your approach - you're probably talking too much.

Follow Up

You've survived your last event, met lots of exciting new people - and yes, a few who you wish had stayed at home! Some of these new people are destined to become close friends and valuable members of your network. Your pockets and luggage are bulging with stacks of their business cards.

Now what? You need a system. Without one, many of these contacts will simply fade in your memory of conferences past. There's simply no point meeting people if you don't have easy access to their most up-to-date contact information.

▶ You have a new hobby - collecting the names and contact details of all the new people you meet.
▶ People change addresses, telephone numbers, and e-mail addresses far more regularly than they did in the past - keep your database up-to-date.
▶ Keeping hundreds of business cards in the bottom

drawer of your desk will seriously undermine your efforts to become well connected!

◗ Add the details of everyone you meet into your computer database or contact management software. Spell their names correctly.

◗ Assign the name of the event to each contact.

◗ Get into the habit of including the notes you wrote about these new people when you met them.

Ways to Re-Connect

◗ E-mail is probably the single most effective means of keeping in touch with people once you have met them. Collect the e-mail addresses of all your friends, family, colleagues, suppliers, customers and everyone you meet.

◗ Apply "The Rule of Four": re-connect with at least four contacts each day - by mail, phone, face-to-face or e-mail. Make it part of your daily routine - it takes very little time.

◗ On your return from events, create a summary of your key learnings, thoughts and insights. Circulate them by e-mail to everyone who you met there and invite additional insights and knowledge nuggets.

◗ If a contact was promised a follow up, do it at the earliest opportunity - you will strengthen your newly created professional, reliable and trustworthy image.

◗ Develop a habit of sending out handwritten 'thank you' notes. This example of good manners has become somewhat rare these days. It is therefore an excellent way to stand out from the crowd.

- If they did a great job, send a handwritten 'thank you' to the host and the organiser of each event you attend.
- Don't contact people only when you want something. They notice. Contact people when you have something valuable to offer. Guess what - more contacts will be pleased to hear from you!
- Once a month, scan through your contacts for people you haven't spoken to in a while. Initiate a call, e-mail or meeting.
- Think more about your contacts. What job opportunities are they looking for? What clients do they want? Become their eyes and ears.

Help - Asking and Offering

- What do you want? Chances are you haven't thought about it that much. Brainstorm all the areas of your life where you might benefit from a bit of help.
- Be open and honest about your needs - no hidden agendas.
- Give help and advice freely with no expectation of a return - don't keep score.
- Return one favour with two or more. This invokes the universal "Law of Reciprocity". More help, opportunities and business will come your way.
- Agree to actively promote the achievements of each other.
- Carry the business cards of those you choose to promote.

Attending a Conference

◗ Make a point of meeting any speakers who particularly interest you BEFORE they speak. Afterwards you will be 'just another face', but beforehand, the most savvy speakers will appreciate any information they can be given about the group, the issues they face, previous speakers and how they were received, the type of questions he/she can expect and any other useful insight you can provide. Succeed at being of value to the speaker in this way and its highly likely you will be mentioned by name during the talk. Speakers like to do that because it helps establish them as someone who is connected to an audience - it wouldn't do your profile any harm either! If you are mentioned, you'll probably find people wanting to talk with you later to agree or discuss the issue further.

◗ Ask if the speaker would appreciate it if you asked a question at the end of the session to stimulate other questions.

◗ If you decide to ask questions of speakers (whether you met them beforehand or not) - 1) Say your name and your company name 2) be brief 3) don't answer the question yourself. (This is also known as showing off)

◗ Identify any industry journalists who may be attending from the delegate list. (Note: Journalists are notorious for not showing up, even after they call to confirm they will be attending.) For leading journalists, look up the publication's website, and search the archive for recent articles by the journalist. Make contact at the event. DO NOT try to sell your company or yourself - everyone tries to persuade journalists to write a story about them. Instead offer to be a resource to them. What are they working on? How could you or your contacts help? Share some of the issues facing colleagues in your industry that haven't been covered in their publication - and why the issues are so important/relevant to their readers.

Attending a Gala Dinner

- Don't change the table plan. Sit where you have been assigned. And make the most of the situation.
- When everyone has arrived and before dinner is served, get up and walk over to those on the other side of your table. Introduce yourself. Find out a little about your fellow diners in the short time you have. Work extra hard at remembering their names for later.
- During the meal speak to those sitting next to you on both sides. Don't focus on only one of them. If you want to extend your conversation to those on the other side of your neighbours - don't talk across that neighbour to reach the person. Ask to be introduced - or offer to introduce them to their other dinner companion.
- If seated next to someone's spouse or partner encourage them to talk about themselves and what interests them. This will help them feel more welcome and ensure they don't have to sit through what is to them, tiresome 'shop talk'.

◗ Some accomplished conversationalists aim to devote their attention to a single person during each course of the meal. When the next course arrives - they turn to their other neighbour. After dessert, before coffee, it is usually acceptable to get up, go elsewhere on your table and pick up your earlier conversation with any of those you met before dinner was served.

Attending Business Meetings

◗ At a meeting of about 12 people, I was particularly impressed with one person who waited to exchange cards once everyone had sat down at the large circular table. He then arranged the cards on the table in front of him, in the same order as those seated around the table. He knew exactly who everybody was and was able to concentrate on the meeting rather than being afraid of addressing someone by the wrong name. A brilliant and simple idea. Use it.

Relationships as Part of a Personal and Professional Strategy

Learning practical tactics and techniques to make the most of being at events has been the primary focus of this book. By applying these ideas your eyes may be opened to the awesome power of a proactive approach to build mutually beneficial relationships.

This short section takes a brief look at how you and your colleagues can benefit from a longer term, more strategic approach. Ask yourself these questions;

- **ID** Who do I and my company need to know (or know better) within the next 12 months?
- **ID** What are my key industry sectors?
- **ID** Who are the key influencers within my target markets/area of interest?
- **ID** What help do they want or need in order to grow their businesses/personal reputation?
- **ID** What do I and my company need to do in order to increase the likelihood that these people will speak well of us to our targeted decision makers?
- **ID** What anxieties and fears do they have in respect of what our company has to offer?
- **ID** Who is able to allay those fears on our behalf?

Let's look a little closer at the first questions. Who do you and your company need to know in the next 12 months? A simple yet profound question that surprisingly few seem able to answer.

Until you can answer this question in a focused, specific way, then your prospective customers and key influencers will remain abstract targets rather than specific individuals. It's always far easier and more effective to get close to one person than to get close to a whole organisation.

When a board of directors of a global insurance firm were asked this question during an in-house executive seminar, they couldn't give me four names. And they weren't even the names of people, but four organisations. One director said "*This is embarrassing. If WE don't know, how can we expect our 8,000 staff."* Good point.

Getting to Know Your Contacts in Five Dimensions

The pre-requisite for mutual benefit is mutual understanding. So, what can you find out about your contacts so that you can help them? Loads of stuff.

1) Who are they? (demographics),
2) What kind of people are they? (psychographics),
3) What social networks or associations are important to them? (sociographics),
4) What do they/their company buy and what's driving these decisions? (value-orientation),
5) How do they buy? (relationship-orientation)

Demographics

1. Name
2. Nickname
3. Job title
4. Since when?
5. Company name
6. Company address
7. Business telephone number
8. Home telephone
9. Business fax
10. Home fax
11. Business e-mail address

12. Personal e-mail
13. Place and date of birth
14. Name of husband, wife or long term partner
15. Children's names (if any)
16. Full name of PA/secretary or assistant
17. Birthday of PA
18. Pets (names and types)
19. Partner's birthday
20. Children's birthdays
21. Academic qualifications
22. Which schools did they go to?
23. Which colleges or universities?
24. Partner's education
25. Subject studied
26. How many times married?
27. Children from previous marriage(s)
28. Who has custody?
29. Wedding anniversary
30. Parents' profession(s)
31. What vehicle does the person drive?
32. Is it personal or company owned?
33. Have they been in the military? If so, when, which regiments, which rank(s)?

Psychographics

34. What are their values? What beliefs shape who they are as a person?
35. How important are money, material possessions, what others think of them, their integrity, reputation, honesty and trust-worthiness?

36. How does their behaviour reinforce or undermine those values?
37. What drives them? Are they trying to prove something to themselves, their family or colleagues?
38. What is their proudest moment?
39. How analytical or practical are they?
40. What books, newspapers, periodicals and magazines do they read?
41. What do they subscribe to? Why?
42. How do they respond to viewpoints different to their own?
43. Who are their role models, heroes and heroines?
44. Who do they most admire in business and in life? Why?
45. Where did they work and for how long in previous organisations?
46. What were their major achievements there?
47. What are their major achievements in their current organisation?
48. Do they have any particular health problems or conditions?
49. What are they doing about solving them?
50. What are their favourite restaurants for lunch or dinner?
51. How well do they work as part of a team?
52. How are they perceived by their colleagues, friends, customers and suppliers?
53. What do they think about the company they work for?
54. What do they want to achieve in the long term - personally as well as professionally?
55. What are their most pressing short-term problems and objectives? (Personally and professionally)

56. How does their perception of customers' problems differ from that of superiors within their organisation?
57. Who are they in conflict with internally and externally?
58. Who are the customers' biggest allies and supporters?
59. Who are the customers' arch rivals? (Personally and professionally)
60. What, if anything, keeps them awake at night through worry? Professional, partner or parenting issues?
61. How forward thinking is the person?
62. What subject areas are taboo with this person?
63. What subject(s) is the person most enthusiastic, passionate about?
64. What subjects are they particularly knowledgeable about?
65. Are they prepared to offer advice on this/these subjects?
66. Who do they want/need to look good in front of?
67. What memorabilia, photographs, awards or executive toys are in their office?
68. What organisational ties, tie-pins or badges do they wear?

Sociographics

69. Where were they brought up?
70. Partner's main interests
71. Children's interests (these change - so stay up-to-date)

72. Who do they most listen to inside and outside the company?
73. Who else within their industry influences their views?
74. What professional or trade associations do they belong to?
75. What are their main interests outside business?
76. What business organisations do they belong to?
77. What social or community organisations do they belong to?
78. How active are they?
79. Which charitable organisations do they support?
80. How do they give their support?
81. Is there a personal reason for this support - perhaps the family member has suffered in some particular way?
82. What political affiliations do they have?
83. What religious affiliations do they have?
84. What other community affiliations do they have?
85. How active are they in these areas?
86. Which organisations do they do voluntary work for?
87. What sports teams do they support?
88. What musical, theatrical, movie and other cultural interests do they have?
89. Who do they know who could provide you with future business possibilities?
90. Why should they share such contacts with you?

Value-Orientation (Corporate Entity)

91. What reputational claims does their company make on their website or in their brochure? Is this congruent/consistent with their behaviour and goals?

92. What issue is absorbing most of their senior management's attention?
93. What type of culture exists within the organisation? What's it like to work there?
94. What is the balance amongst employees between anxiety and hope?
95. How highly is the company regarded by suppliers, customers and other stakeholders?
96. What are their stakeholders saying behind their back?
97. What qualities and attributes do they look for in suppliers?
98. Who are their top suppliers and why?

Relationship-Orientation (Corporate Entity)

99. How loyal is this customer to you and your company?
100. What is this loyalty or lack of loyalty based on?
101. What can be done to improve the customer's loyalty and trust?
102. Do they already have a successful partnership with another firm?
103. How frequently do they change suppliers and why?
104. If they hold beauty parades - how many contestants are there?
105. Which of your prospects are most accepting of the benefits of long-term relationships?
106. Which of your prospects are most resistant to the idea of long-term partnerships?

Originally based on the Mackay Envelope Corporation 66-Question Customer Profile.

Beware, information such as this is subject to the UK's Data Protection Act. For more information, visit www.DataProtection.gov.uk to find out how this could affect you.

Note that some of the above information is time sensitive - keep it up-to-date. People move jobs, split up, divorce and die. A well-meaning anniversary card to someone whose partner died a few years before will hardly improve your relationship.

In Summary

Ideas, tactics and techniques to help you gain the most from attending events has been the aim of this little pocket book. I hope it has given you much food for thought and addressed most of the issues faced by business people when called upon to work a room. If you wish to bring to our attention any omissions that could be included in future editions - e-mail me at Roy@RoySpeaks.com. Any ideas used will be credited to the first person to contact me.

With a little thought and a desire to reach out to new people, you can get really GREAT at this. And have a lot of fun in the process. Teach this stuff to your colleagues and contacts - the more people who know the rules of this contact sport, the more you will benefit. Good luck.

It has been said that strangers are only friends you haven't met yet. And it's worth remembering what Ralph Waldo Emerson said *"If you want a friend, be one."*

Meet Greet and Prosper Reminders

- ⅠⅠ Be Proactive. Decide to "Get out more."
- ⅠⅠ Seek ways to be of value to those you meet.
- ⅠⅠ Be clear about what help you can offer others and what help you would appreciate.
- ⅠⅠ Who do you want to know in the next 12 months?
- ⅠⅠ Make a point of meeting more NEW people, instead of just sticking with those you feel most comfortable with.
- ⅠⅠ When introduced, imagine you will have to introduce this new person to someone else within the next 10 minutes - so pay more attention!
- ⅠⅠ Be interested. Don't worry about being interesting.
- ⅠⅠ Develop a memorable self-introduction that focusses on the results you help to create.
- ⅠⅠ Ask gentle, insightful questions of those you meet and really listen to what is said.
- ⅠⅠ Memorise the questions on pages 29 and 30.
- ⅠⅠ Take the initiative to bring conversations to a close by being honest about wanting to meet others.
- ⅠⅠ Collect the contact details of everyone you meet.
- ⅠⅠ Apply the "Rule of Four" by re-connecting with four people every day - especially when you don't want something.
- ⅠⅠ Enjoy yourself!

About the Author

Roy Sheppard is an international business speaker and world-class conference moderator and link presenter for some of the largest and most successful global organisations. He is an acknowledged expert on building profitable business relationships through networking and referrals.

Author of the best selling book *Rapid Result Referrals*, the first chapter is available as a free download: www.RoySpeaks.com/rrr.htm

He conducts seminars, in-house company workshops and keynote speeches at conferences all over the world. Roy could be a valuable and entertaining addition to your next conference or meeting.

Contact:

Centre Publishing, Croft House, Clapton, Midsomer Norton, Bath, Somerset BA3 4EB England.
Tel: 00 44 (0) 1761 414676
Fax: 00 44 (0) 1761 412615
Email: Roy@RoySpeaks.com
Web: http://www.RoySpeaks.com, with streaming video.

If you have found this book to be useful, please don't keep it a secret. Tell your contacts about it. Thanks. It can be ordered on-line at a special rate that includes free postage and packing to any full postal address in the world.

Visit www.RoySpeaks.com/mgp.htm for details.

Recommended Reading

For an up-to-date list of recommended books and other learning materials on this and related topics,

Visit www.RoySpeaks.com/greet.htm

Attract More Quality Clients Discreetly - Without Selling

Rapid Result Referrals by Roy Sheppard

How you will benefit from this book

ID Acquire more quality clients in less time and earn more

ID Learn how to turn your clients into raving fans

ID Enhance your personal and professional reputation

ID Find out exactly how the most successful businesses quietly capture clients under the noses of their competitors

ID Over a hundred creative, profit-producing ideas and step-by-step guidance on how to implement similar strategies for your own business

Its bullet point format and no waffle style takes you right to the bottom line and provides the vital information you need, as you need it.

"A huge number of practical business generating ideas with an enthusiastic 'can-do' style .... a must read book." Eric Peacock, Chairman, Business Link Hertfordshire, England

"Sheppard has forged highly practical and effective tools for growth .... You know instinctively that the ideas will work. I commend this book." Marion Royer, London Chamber of Commerce and Industry, England

"Anybody who wants to grow their business should read this book. It provides the nutrients needed for growth. Roy Sheppard has given me business advice which works. All I can say is read it and do it." Chris Moon, MBE International Speaker, mine clearance campaigner and author of "One Step Beyond"

"Roy Sheppard gives a compelling insight into what works in business. I have known Roy for some years, and he cares about people, their ideas and their vision. His sincerity shines through in all that he does. I thoroughly recommend that you listen to what this man has to say." Lord Taylor of Warwick

160 pages ISBN 1-901-53404-9 Paperback

For Imaginative Event Organisers

Events, conference, seminars, trade shows and exhibitions cost an absolute fortune to stage. Organisers need to ensure they gain a return on their considerable investment. Helping delegates make the most of networking opportunities is a great way to ensure they receive value from attending. This improves the effectiveness of the event. So everyone wins.

Why not send a customised copy of *Meet, Greet and Prosper* to each delegate ahead of your next event? Or include it as part of their delegate pack. Some companies send it out as a corporate gift to thank their customers for their business.

The cover of *Meet, Greet and Prosper* can be customised with your company colours, name and logo. Inside, we can also include a personal message from a sponsor or a key executive. At an affordable price.

For a quotation based on your specific requirements, email Adrie@RoySpeaks.com.